HAUNTED PLACES

HAUNTED SHIPS & LIGHTHOUSES

by Heather C. Hudak

BrightPoint Press

San Diego, CA

BrightPoint Press

an imprint of ReferencePoint Press, Inc.
Printed in the United States

For more information, contact:
BrightPoint Press
PO Box 27779
San Diego, CA 92198
www.BrightPointPress.com

LIBRARY OF CONGRESS CATALOGING-IN-PUBLICATION DATA

Name: Hudak, Heather C., author.
Title: Haunted ships & lighthouses / by Heather C. Hudak.
Description: San Diego, CA: ReferencePoint Press, 2026 | Series: Haunted places | Audience: Grade 7 to 9 | Includes bibliographical references and index.
Identifiers: ISBN: 9781678211868 (hardcover) | ISBN: 9781678211875 (eBook)
The complete Library of Congress record is available at www.loc.gov.

CONTENTS

AT A GLANCE

- Some people report unexplained experiences at ships and lighthouses. They believe these places might be haunted.

- The spirits of people who died in shipwrecks, during sea storms, or in pirate attacks are said to haunt ships and lighthouses.

- Electrical energy generated by water and lightning storms is said to attract ghosts. Some people believe they use the energy to manifest.

- Ships found floating at sea with no one aboard are called ghost ships. They are often the subject of stories about spirits lost at sea.

- People have been fascinated by the paranormal for centuries. Many claim to have firsthand accounts of spirits haunting ships and lighthouses.

- Ghost hunters are also called paranormal investigators. They use special equipment to search for ghosts in places that are thought to be haunted.

- Many supposedly haunted ships and lighthouses in the United States were made into museums or hotels. People can take paranormal tours or stay overnight at these places.

- No one knows for sure whether ghosts are real, but people still look for evidence of hauntings.

CREEPY CABIN

Julie Tremaine was a ghost hunter. In 2019, she was part of a **paranormal** investigation. The group was investigating on the RMS *Queen Mary*. This ship was docked in Long Beach, California. It was an ocean liner that operated during the mid-1900s. It was made into a hotel in 1972.

Tremaine and the team spent the evening in room B340. Guests had reported strange activity there. This included claims of

Construction of the RMS *Queen Mary* began in 1930 in Clydebank, Scotland.

QUEEN MARY

The *Queen Mary* is about 1,020 feet (311 m) long and has more than 300 rooms on board.

seeing ghosts. Tremaine and the team felt as though they were not alone in the room. They said they captured the voices of spirits on their audio recorders. One seemed to say, "Hassle."

Later, the team started packing up. One investigator asked Tremaine whether she would spend the night alone in B340. She said yes. The team set up a video camera in the room. After everyone left, Tremaine went to bed. But she had trouble falling asleep. Then, she started hearing voices. At first, she thought it was other guests walking the halls. But something did not feel right.

The next morning, Tremaine reviewed the video footage. She noticed a stick-like figure standing over her. She also heard "Hassle" again on her recorder. But it sounded much louder. She thought it came from the figure in the video. Tremaine said, "Even totally alone . . . I made it through to the morning. Scratch that: I wasn't alone—there

Ships and lighthouses are some of the many locations around the world that people believe are haunted.

was just no other living person in the room with me."[1]

HAUNTINGS AT SEA AND BEYOND

Throughout history, people have told chilling tales of disasters at sea. These stories are often surrounded by mystery. Some are about ships that disappeared, sank, or were abandoned. Others are about spooky experiences at lighthouses.

The *Queen Mary* is one of many supposedly haunted ships and lighthouses in the United States. Some people report strange sights and sounds at these places. They say the spirits of passengers, sailors, and workers haunt ships and lighthouses.

CHAPTER ONE

SUPERNATURAL FORCES

Some people believe water attracts ghosts. Lightning storms and moving water create electrical energy in the air. Ghosts are said to use energy to connect with the living world. This is why there are so many stories about haunted ships and lighthouses.

Zak Bagans is a paranormal investigator. He stars on the television show *Ghost Adventures*. Bagans talked about how

People have been telling ghostly sea stories for hundreds of years.

Lighthouses use bright lights and loud horns to help ships navigate through fog.

spirits use energy. He said, "Spirits . . . are not capable of **manifesting** themselves into sound or sight until they come in contact with a greater amount of energy that they can borrow or take altogether."[2]

WHY LIGHTHOUSES ARE HAUNTED

Lighthouses are buildings near water. Their purpose is to guide ships. They use light to help ships navigate in dangerous water or storms. People who watch over lighthouses are called keepers. Keepers stand watch over the waters day and night.

There are many reasons lighthouses are commonly believed to be haunted. They are close to water. They are surrounded by energy. Lighthouses are built to withstand strong winds and storms. These weather conditions also generate energy. Some people think this energy attracts **supernatural** forces. They claim spirits can use this energy to show themselves.

Sometimes the light from the lighthouse was not enough to help ships reach shore. The conditions at sea might have been too rough. Or sailors did not see the light in time. Ships would hit rocks or other obstacles. This could have caused them to sink. Because of this, lighthouses are often associated with tragedy and death. Some people believe this makes them more likely to be haunted.

Spirits are also believed to haunt places where they have emotional ties. Lighthouses are often far from towns or other people. Lighthouse keepers might have had little or no contact with people for weeks at a time. Many became lonely. Sometimes, the sadness was too much, driving the lighthouse keeper to take extreme actions. There are chilling tales of keepers who went mad or disappeared. Some died by suicide. Others even murdered their families. The keepers' ghosts are said to haunt the lighthouses.

WHY SHIPS ARE HAUNTED

Like lighthouses, ships are surrounded by water. Ships often face rough waves and powerful storms. These conditions create energy. People claim spirits use energy to interact with the physical world. This is one reason why ships might attract ghosts.

Another reason is the vastness of the open ocean. It has always been a place

Mary Celeste

The *Mary Celeste* is one of the most famous spooky ships. In November 1872, the ship set sail from New York for Italy. It was found floating near islands in the North Atlantic Ocean a few weeks later. There was no one aboard. Many people claimed the *Mary Celeste* was haunted. Sailors also reported seeing ghostly figures in the waters near where it was found.

of mystery, danger, and adventure. Sailors could die while at sea. This might have been from diseases or natural disasters. Or they died from battles and pirate attacks. There are also tales of murder and disappearances aboard ships. People claim ships are haunted by those who died aboard.

Some ships have been found floating at sea. They have no crew or passengers aboard. These are known as ghost ships. Ghost ships are mysteries. No one knows why the people on the ship disappeared. Some ghost ships go missing for years. But they are often in good condition when they are found. Ghost ships spark stories of lost souls haunting the seas.

Eve Church is a writer. She wrote an article on ghost ships. She said, "These mysterious vessels remind us of the vast, unpredictable power of the sea and the dangers that lurk within its depths."[3]

Ghost ships could have been abandoned for a variety of reasons, including bad weather, mechanical problems, or pirates.

CHAPTER TWO

SPOOKY ENCOUNTERS

For centuries, people have been fascinated by the paranormal. Many people claim to have unusual experiences at haunted ships and lighthouses. They give eyewitness accounts of strange sights and sounds. They believe ghosts are haunting these places.

The Yaquina Bay Lighthouse is located in Newport, Oregon. The lighthouse was built in 1871. It shut down just 3 years later.

The Yaquina Bay Lighthouse is the only historic wooden lighthouse in Oregon.

Since then, people have reported unexplained events there. These include mysterious lights outside the lighthouse on foggy nights.

Unexplained footsteps, sudden temperature changes, and shadowy figures are common reports at places believed to be haunted.

In 1899, a woman named Lischen Miller wrote a story about the Yaquina Bay Lighthouse. The story was published in a magazine. It was about a girl named Muriel Trevenard. Her father left her with a couple living at a nearby house while he went out to sea. Muriel and her friends decided to explore the abandoned lighthouse. They got scared when the fog came in. So they left.

Muriel had left a handkerchief inside. She returned to get it. She never returned. "There were blood drops in the hall and on the stairs that led up to the landing, and in the linen closet they picked up a bloodstained handkerchief. But there was nothing else," Miller wrote.[4] Muriel's father never returned to learn about his daughter.

Today, people claim to see the shadowy figure of a young woman in the lighthouse window. She is said to be waving a handkerchief. Some say they hear Muriel's ghost screaming for help on foggy nights.

PLYMOUTH LIGHT

Plymouth Light is located in Plymouth, Massachusetts. It is also known as the Gurnet Light. It was first built in 1768. Local people rented the land from John Thomas. He was then assigned as the first keeper. John died in 1776. His wife, Hannah, became the keeper. Some people claim that Hannah's spirit still roams the grounds. She is said to be looking for her husband.

Sandra and Bob Shanklin are lighthouse photographers. They spent the night at Plymouth Light. Bob experienced something strange during the stay. He woke up in the middle of the night. He claimed to see the head and shoulders of a woman floating above Sandra. Bob did not feel threatened by the figure. But he did sense sadness coming from her.

Bob turned to look at the light from the lighthouse shining through the window. When he turned back, the figure

Hannah Thomas

Hannah Thomas was the first female lighthouse keeper in the United States. She took over the role when her husband, John, died during the American Revolutionary War (1775–1783). Hannah worked alone in the lighthouse until 1786. In 1790, the lighthouse was turned over to the US government.

Plymouth Light had two lights until 1924, when one of them was shut down.

had disappeared. Other people have also reported seeing Hannah's spirit.

SS *VALENCIA*

In 1906, the passenger ship SS *Valencia* set sail from San Francisco, California. It was headed to Seattle, Washington. The ship sailed through bad weather. It hit a reef near Vancouver Island, Canada. A large hole in the side of the ship caused it to sink. Rough waters made it hard for those aboard to use lifeboats. Rescue attempts were unsuccessful due to the stormy seas and rocky cliffs.

Only thirty-seven of the 173 aboard the ship survived. Months later, one of the ship's lifeboats was found near shore. But there were only skeletons inside. Since then, people have reported seeing lifeboats floating mysteriously in the ocean near where the skeletons were found.

The sinking of the *Valencia* is one of the worst sea disasters along the West Coast. Some people believe those who died onboard still haunt the waters. Stories include sightings of a **phantom** ship sailing in the area. The ship is said to be crewed by skeletons. Figures are said to clinging to the ship's ropes.

The SS *Valencia* was built in Philadelphia, Pennsylvania, in 1882.

In 1910, sailors said they saw a ship similar to the *Valencia* stuck in rocks. But it disappeared as they approached. In 1933, one of the ship's lifeboats was said to be found. It seemed in almost perfect condition despite being lost at sea for nearly 30 years. The boat had no human remains in it.

GHOST SHIP OF THE NORTHUMBERLAND STRAIT

In eastern Canada, tales about the Ghost Ship of the Northumberland Strait date back about 200 years. The ship is one of the most famous ghost ships in North America. But its origins remain unknown. Some people believe it was a French warship in the 1700s. The crew might have set the ship on fire to avoid being captured.

Others think that the ship was simply lost at sea.

People have claimed to see a large ship on fire in the water. Some reports include sightings of a ghostly crew trying to put out the flames. The ship is sometimes seen before a storm or at night.

In the 1970s, author Sterling Ramsay wrote a book. It is called *Folklore, Prince Edward Island*. He describes a sighting of the ghost ship. Ramsey wrote:

> *A group of men boarded a small boat and rowed toward the flaming ship, in hopes of rescuing as many of her crew as possible. While they were still some distance from the craft, it disappeared into the mist and appeared to vanish completely.*[5]

The ghosts of crew members who died are sometimes said to haunt the ships they worked on.

Many people are interested in stories like these. They want to know whether ghosts are real. Some people investigate supposedly haunted lighthouses and ships. They search for proof of the paranormal.

CHAPTER THREE

HUNTING FOR HAUNTS

Ghost hunters investigate places that are said to be haunted. These people are also called paranormal investigators. They travel to haunted locations. They use special equipment to look for evidence of ghosts. This equipment includes **infrared** cameras, **electromagnetic** field (EMF) detectors, and spirit boxes.

The Fire Island Lighthouse was built in 1858. It is on Fire Island in New York.

Paranormal investigators use ghost hunting equipment to try to detect the presence of spirits and record unexplained sounds and voices.

Many people claim it is haunted by a former keeper and his daughter. Stories say the daughter fell sick. She died before a doctor could arrive. The keeper hung himself out of guilt over her death. Sightings of a shadowy male figure are reported at the lighthouse.

The Fire Island Lighthouse is 168 feet (51 m) tall.

In January 2022, seven ghost hunters investigated the lighthouse. They claimed to capture evidence of spirits. One video seemed to show part of a figure. It disappeared into the lighthouse's gift shop. The investigators also recorded audio of a woman's voice. They believed it was the voice of Margaret Fuller. Fuller was an author during the 1800s. She died in a shipwreck near Fire Island.

ABSECON LIGHTHOUSE

In 1854, a ship called the USS *Powhatan* sank near Long Beach, New York. Around 300 people died. Many of the bodies washed ashore farther south. This included the area near Absecon, New Jersey.

The Absecon Lighthouse was built soon after the accident. Today, it is said to be haunted by the spirits of those who died in the shipwreck. Some people have reported seeing ghostly figures. Others have claimed to hear unexplained voices. Some people also report smelling cigar smoke.

The Atlantic Paranormal Society (TAPS) is featured on the show *Ghost Hunters*. In 2009, TAPS visited the Absecon Lighthouse. During the investigation, the team asked if anyone was with them in the lighthouse. The recorder captured unexplained voices. A camera also appeared to move on its own. That same camera captured video of a shadowy figure.

TAPS found explanations for some of the reported activity. The investigators had

Ghost hunters often use cameras to help them capture evidence in the dark.

visited during a storm. Strong winds made the windows rattle. They believed that caused the unexplained noises. They also thought the wind could carry the sounds of people talking at the bottom of the stairs. That could have been the source of the reported voices.

USS *THE SULLIVANS*

USS *The Sullivans* is a US Navy ship. It was named after five brothers who were killed fighting in World War II (1939–1945).

USS *The Sullivans* was originally called the USS *Putnam*. It was renamed in 1943.

The ship was docked in Buffalo, New York, in 1977. It was turned into a museum.

Reports of paranormal experiences on the ship started in the 1960s when it was first taken out of service. A shadowy figure is said to patrol the ship's lower decks. It is believed to be George, the oldest Sullivan brother. A photo honoring the brothers is displayed on the ship. When people take pictures of it, George's face does not appear clearly.

In 2014, the ship was featured on *Ghost Hunters*. During the investigation, three TAPS members heard footsteps. They also recorded unexplained voices, whistling, and knocking sounds.

At another point, investigators heard what sounded like a door closing.

Steve Gonsalves was an investigator with TAPS. He said:

> *After we heard that, we actually went around quite extensively to try to find a door that would make that sound, but if they were open, they were latched, so that they couldn't move. . . . So, that was a little peculiar for us not being able to find the origin of that sound.*[6]

Spirit Box

Ghost hunters use a tool called a spirit box. It is a device that quickly scans radio stations. It creates a mix of sounds and signals called white noise. Ghost hunters claim spirits can use the energy from white noise to form words. It allows spirits to communicate with the living.

Thermometers allow paranormal investigators to check for sudden temperature changes, which could indicate the presence of a spirit.

RMS *QUEEN MARY*

The RMS *Queen Mary* is considered one of the most haunted ships in the world. From 1936 to 1967, it carried about 3 million people across the Atlantic Ocean. Dozens of people died on the ship during this time. Their ghosts are said to still haunt the ship.

Many places on the *Queen Mary* are believed to be haunted, including Room B340, the swimming pool, and the Queen's Salon.

Ghost hunters from around the world visit the ship. They hope to encounter some of the spirits onboard. One of those ghosts is believed to be John Pedder. Pedder was a crew member on the ship. In 1966, the 18-year-old was crushed by a door onboard. Since then, many people have claimed to see his ghost.

In 2014, the *Queen Mary* was featured on an episode of *Ghost Adventures*. Zak Bagans and his crew led the investigation. They used a recording device to try to capture electronic voice phenomena (EVP). These are ghostly voices. The group also claimed to see orbs of light floating around. A camera captured a shadowy figure crossing a doorway.

Many ghost hunters have investigated reports of unexplained activity. But there is no proof that places such as ships and lighthouses are haunted. Even so, ghost hunters continue to look for explanations for people's paranormal experiences.

CHAPTER FOUR

TOURING THE SCENE

Many supposedly haunted ships and lighthouses in the United States are open to the public. Some are museums. They share their history with visitors. Others are hotels where people can stay overnight. These places might offer tours or host events related to their haunted history. Some even let guests take part in their own paranormal investigations.

Many people go on haunted tours in the hopes of witnessing something paranormal.

Saint Augustine Lighthouse is in Saint Augustine, Florida. It is said to be one of the oldest and most haunted buildings in

Saint Augustine, Florida, was founded in 1565. It is the oldest city in the United States.

the United States. Some people claim the lighthouse is haunted by several spirits. These include the ghosts of two former lighthouse keepers. The spirits of three girls who drowned are said to haunt there, too.

Today, the lighthouse is a museum. Daily tours are offered. Sometimes, the lighthouse has after-dark experiences. These events showcase the lighthouse's haunted history.

The Dark Moon Tour allows guests to visit the lighthouse, its grounds, and the keeper's house. It takes place at night. Guests are given a glow stick to help light their way. They can also rent an EMF detector. During the tour, guides tell stories of ghostly experiences at the lighthouse.

Jayda Barnes once visited the lighthouse. She talked about a spooky experience she had on the tour. “One man sat in one of the resident ghost’s favorite chairs,” Barnes said. “As the guest spoke to the room, EMF meters began lighting up red around his shoulders, indicating some paranormal activity. The more we spoke and scanned the room, the more lights lit up.”[7]

Haunted History

Saint Augustine is the oldest city in the United States. It was founded in 1565 by a Spanish explorer. Many people believe it is one of the most haunted US cities. A number of places in the city are said to be haunted. This includes the Saint Augustine Lighthouse. Other places that might be haunted are the Old Jail, Huguenot Cemetery, and the Spanish Military Hospital Museum.

MARQUETTE HARBOR LIGHTHOUSE

Marquette Harbor Lighthouse is on the shore of Lake Superior in Michigan. It was originally built in the mid-1800s. The spirits of people who died in shipwrecks are believed to haunt the lighthouse.

The Marquette Maritime Museum hosts guided tours. Visitors can learn about the haunted history of both the lighthouse and the area. One story is about a body that was found frozen in ice. Two fingers came off when the body was removed. Some people claim they have felt a three-fingered hand touch their shoulder when walking along the shore.

Visitors to the lighthouse are also able to do their own investigations. They can

Some people have reported seeing the ghost of a little girl at the Marquette Harbor Lighthouse.

use real ghost hunting equipment. They can look for evidence of hauntings. Susan Hill is a tour guide at the lighthouse. She talked about hearing unexplained footsteps while giving tours. "I didn't actually believe in ghosts before I started volunteering here, and now I most definitely do beyond a shadow of a doubt," said Hill.[8]

USS *HORNET*

The USS *Hornet* is a retired aircraft carrier with a haunted history. It is docked in Alameda, California. During World War II, the USS *Hornet* carried aircraft and crew members into battle on the Pacific Ocean. In 1969, the ship was used to pick up astronauts after missions to the moon.

Today, the *Hornet* is a museum. Many people say the ship is haunted. Some have reported tables moving and lights flickering. Others say they heard the sounds of gunfire, footsteps, and voices.

Shadowy figures wandering the halls have also been reported. One is known as the Dress Whites Ghost. He is believed to be a sailor. He is spotted wearing a white uniform.

Bob Eiess is a volunteer on the *Hornet*. He experienced something strange while aboard. "I saw what I thought was one of my coworkers stepping off the main hall onto a side passage," Eiess said. "I called out to him, but he kept walking and when I got to the hall he stepped into, there was a chain blocking the entrance, and it was an empty compartment."[9]

The *Hornet* hosts after-hours events where guests can stay overnight. Guides take visitors on an investigation of the most haunted areas of the ship. Those who

In 1991, the USS *Hornet* was made into a US National Historic Landmark.

dare can stay the night in the former crew quarters.

A girl and her friends once stayed overnight on the ship. She was resting on a bunk bed. Suddenly, she felt someone pushing up on it. But she was alone. The girl claimed to see two ghostly faces of sailors in the darkness. One of them said, "Watch that one." Then, they faded away.

USS *SALEM*

The USS *Salem* is a museum in Quincy, Massachusetts. In 1953, a huge earthquake hit islands off the coast of Greece. The ship

Guests can go on guided or self-guided tours of the USS *Salem*.

served as a makeshift hospital. It also had a **morgue**. It was said to have held around 400 victims.

Some people say the ghosts of those who died onboard still haunt the ship. Strange sights, smells, and sounds have been reported. The ship's dining hall is believed to have the most paranormal activity. It is located above the morgue.

One spirit on the ship is called the Burning Man. He is said to smell like death. The Burning Man is believed to be a victim of the earthquake. He is sometimes seen during tours. He is spotted in a room that was once the ship's morgue. Some people believe that is where he died.

Guests can do a paranormal investigation on the *Salem*. Ghost hunters from the

Greater Boston Paranormal Associates act as guides. Guests can use ghost hunting equipment to search for spirits.

Death and despair are common on the open seas. This can be due to shipwrecks, deadly storms, and battles. Many people claim to have seen or heard strange things when visiting ships and lighthouses. Some even search for evidence of hauntings. Although there is no proof that ghosts are real, unexplained events continue to give people the chills.

FAMOUS HAUNTED SHIPS AND LIGHTHOUSES IN THE UNITED STATES

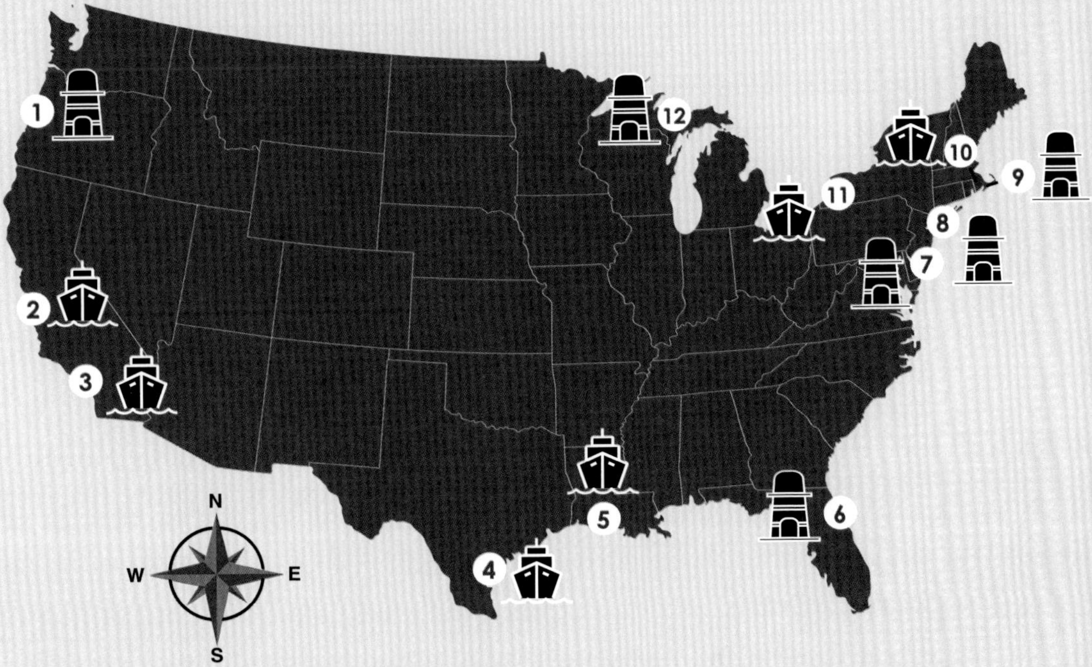

1. Yaquina Bay Lighthouse: Newport, Oregon
2. USS *Hornet*: Alameda, California
3. RMS *Queen Mary*: Long Beach, California
4. USS *Lexington*: Corpus Christi, Texas
5. USS *Kidd*: Baton Rouge, Louisiana
6. Saint Augustine Lighthouse: Saint Augustine, Florida
7. Absecon Lighthouse: Atlantic City, New Jersey
8. Fire Island Lighthouse: Fire Island, New York
9. Plymouth Light: Plymouth, Massachusetts
10. USS *Salem*: Quincy, Massachusetts
11. USS *The Sullivans*: Buffalo, New York
12. Marquette Harbor Lighthouse: Marquette, Michigan

Many old ships and lighthouses across the United States are believed to be haunted.

GLOSSARY

electromagnetic

having to do with a relationship between electricity and magnetic fields

infrared

a type of light that humans cannot see

manifesting

appearing or becoming visible to the human eye

morgue

a place where dead bodies are kept

paranormal

something that is unexplained by science, such as ghosts or aliens

phantom

a ghost or spirit

supernatural

something that cannot be explained by natural laws or science

SOURCE NOTES

INTRODUCTION: CREEPY CABIN

1. Julie Tremaine, "I Stayed in California's Most Haunted Hotel Room," *Syfy*, April 17, 2019. www.syfy.com.

CHAPTER ONE: SUPERNATURAL FORCES

2. Quoted in "Zak Bagans Quotes," *Goodreads*, n.d. www.goodreads.com.

3. Eve Church, "The Mysterious World of Ghost Ships & Some Famous Examples," *Martide*, October 31, 2024. www.martide.com.

CHAPTER TWO: SPOOKY ENCOUNTERS

4. Quoted in "The Haunted Light at Newport-by-the-Sea," *Offbeat Oregon*, n.d. www.offbeatoregon.com.

5. Quoted in "The Ghost Ship of the Northumberland Strait," *Fox Harb'r*, June 18, 2020. www.foxharbr.com.

CHAPTER THREE: HUNTING FOR HAUNTS

6. Quoted in "Ghost Hunters – Phantom Fleet," *Dailymotion*, July 19, 2017. www.dailymotion.com.

CHAPTER FOUR: TOURING THE SCENE

7. Jayda Barnes, "Ghost Tour Experience," *St. Augustine Lighthouse & Maritime Museum*, November 8, 2018. www.staugustinelighthouse.org.

8. Quoted in "Ghosts of Lighthouse Point," *Marquette Maritime Museum*, 2025. www.mqtmaritimemuseum.com.

9. Quoted in "USS Hornet Ghost Stories," *Caltech*, n.d. https://its.caltech.edu.

FOR FURTHER RESEARCH

BOOKS

Heather Alexander, *Haunted USA: Spine-Tingling Stories from All 50 States*. Wide Eyed Editions, 2025.

Insha Fitzpatrick, *Chilling with Ghosts: A Totally Factual Field Guide to the Supernatural*. Quirk Books, 2023.

Laura Stickney, *Haunted Hotels*. BrightPoint Press, 2026.

INTERNET SOURCES

"Maine's Most Haunted Lighthouses," *American Ghost Walks*, September 13, 2022. www.americanghostwalks.com.

"The Ghosts of St. Augustine Lighthouse," *Ghost City Tours*, n.d. https://ghostcitytours.com.

"The Spookiest Ghost Ship Stories from Around the World," *Boat International*, n.d. www.boatinternational.com.

WEBSITES

Ghosts and Gravestones

www.ghostsandgravestones.com

The Ghosts and Gravestones site offers information on haunted locations across the United States. The site features several haunted ships and lighthouses along with tours that people can go on at those places.

Haunted US

https://hauntedus.com

The Haunted US site explores a variety of haunted places, including ships and lighthouses. People can search for haunted locations in each US state and learn more about the paranormal activity people have reported at those places.

The *Queen Mary*

www.queenmary.com

This site features information on the RMS *Queen Mary*. People can learn about the haunted history of the ship and explore the different ghost tours offered onboard.

INDEX

IMAGE CREDITS

Cover: © Cliff Self/Shutterstock Images
5: © MilaCroft/Shutterstock Images
7: © Carol M. Highsmith/Library of Congress
8: © Paul R. Jones/Shutterstock Images
10: © Raggedstone/Shutterstock Images
13: © Ysbrand Cosijn/Shutterstock Images
14: © janars/Shutterstock Images
19: © Dino Osmic/Shutterstock Images
21: © Manuela Durson/Shutterstock Images
22: © jgolby/Shutterstock Images
26: © Michael Sean O'Leary/Shutterstock Images
28: © Historic Collection/Alamy
31: © whitemay/iStockphoto
33: © Stuart Villanueva/The Galveston County Daily News/AP Images
34: © Tyler Kuliberda/National Park Service
37: © Georgiy Datsenko/iStockphoto
38: © US Navy/Naval History and Heritage Command
41: © Juiced Up Media/Shutterstock Images
42: © Paul R. Jones/Shutterstock Images
45: © Viaval Tours/Shutterstock Images
46: © Neflo Photo/Shutterstock Images
50: © John McCormick/Shutterstock Images
53: © DreamArt123/Shutterstock Images
54: © Yingna Cai/Shutterstock Images
57 (lighthouses): © phipatbig/Shutterstock Images
57 (ships): © blinkblink/Shutterstock Images
57 (map): © Red Line Editorial

ABOUT THE AUTHOR

Heather C. Hudak has written hundreds of books for young people on various topics. When she's not writing, Heather loves to travel. On one memorable occasion, she stayed in the hotel on the *Queen Mary*. She took an after-hours ghost tour that included a visit to cabin B340. She didn't see any ghosts, but she felt a creepy energy that made her spine tingle.